PERFECTING THE LIFESTYLE CALLED PUNCTUALITY

Become time-conscious before it's too late

Jeremy Bolton

"Promptitude is not only a duty, but is also a part of good manners; it is favorable to fortune, reputation, influence, and usefulness; a little attention and energy will form the habit, so as to make it easy and delightful."

— Charles Simmons

"I have noticed that the people who are late are often so much jollier than the people who have to wait for them."

— Edward Verrall Lucas

"The Lord is the greatest of all believers in punctuality. In fact, he is the author of punctuality. He has a billion planets whirling through space in different directions and at different speeds, but each one is exactly on time. If one planet were a half minute late there might be very serious consequences. But God, who is the author of order, is in the habit of having his creations in exactly the right places at exactly the right time. Then how do you think he must feel when his greatest masterpiece, created in his own image, shows a high degree of irresponsibility and undependability in keeping his most simple appointments?"

— Sterling W. Sill

"Arriving late was a way of saying that your own time was more valuable than the time of the person who waited for you."

— Karen Joy Fowler, The Jane Austen Book Club

CONTENTS

INTRODUCTION

Don't Waste my Time!

We have been able to conquer virtually everything that life has thrown at us and we seem to be in control of almost everything, from our family life to our career and job. However, there is one thing we all never seem to be able to control, no matter how hard we try. That thing is time.

Time keeps ticking away regardless of what we do or don't do. It is the one thing we can't stop, pause, rewind or fast forward; we can only live in the moment and try as much as possible to somewhat manage it. Your time is therefore a valuable asset, more valuable than even money, and you need to use it very wisely. For most of us, the way we utilize our time has already been made up for us. We have a regular schedule that is quite predictable, from the time we get out of bed, to the time we get to work and then get back home. We don't even think about it; it's just like clockwork - 06:00 AM - out of bed, 08:00 AM - out of the house, 08:45 AM - at work, 17:00 PM - out of the office, 18:00 PM - back home; sounds familiar?! Most people have a regular routine and quite frankly, they get irritated when their routine is obstructed in any way and you really can't blame them. It's just part of our make-up, our DNA if you like. You often hear statements like - "don't waste my time!", "My time is precious!" or my personal favorite, "I don't have the time!" This mindset tends to make us prioritize our time based on our needs and our interests. While it is good to prioritize your time, you also need to know that you are not some lone survivor from a capsized boat on a remote deserted island. You are a human being living in a community with family, friends and colleagues, all living and working together with both individual and collective goals. So your time, as precious as it is, is not completely yours to play with. You have other commitments that take up other people's time as well, so you have to respect that. As you stay true to your own regular routine, you need to remember that your wife and kids at home also need your attention and time, your boss at work can have a hold of your time as he pays your wages, and ultimately, as precious as your time is, it may not absolutely be yours to begin with.

Sharing your Time!

Once you are over the "your time is precious" mantra, you begin to realize that the time you believed was completely yours actually partly belongs to others. The onus is on you to manage it appropriately so that everyone's happy, yourself included. Our ability to share our precious time with those directly or indirectly connected to our lives is what makes us human, but sharing our time also means being able to respect the time of others, and that means being punctual in everything we do. Yes, I know you are a busy executive, but your wife needs you to pick up the kids from school at lunch time. Instead, you decide to do more work and you completely forget or you arrive at your kids' school quite late. One thing for sure, you will have a cold dinner waiting for you when you get home. Sharing your time means being organized and knowing that you have other obligations to meet, other than your own. It also means you have a duty to respect the time of others and stop being selfish with your time. More light can be placed on the scenario stated earlier. You completely fail to pick your kids from their school at your lunch and free time, even though it was the plan you had made with your wife all along. This forces your wife to change her plans and adjust her time in order to pick up the kids from school and make up for your self-indulgence. Sharing your time doesn't mean an infringement on your privacy. It simply means you are well organized and you use your valuable time well. It also means that you appreciate and respect the time of others, and you are willing to sacrifice your time in order to fulfill an obligation.

You are Late!

Quite often, we have a ready-made excuse for why we are unable to keep to time. "Oh, I was busy" or "I had a tight schedule". Another very popular one is "I was stuck in traffic". Whatever reason you have for not being punctual, the bottom line is - you were late. Now I'm not saying that there are not circumstances that are beyond our control that could make us late for a scheduled appointment. It happens, right?! What is alarming however is when your lateness for virtually every occasion is a no-brainer. When it gets to a point where bets are made on how late you would be, then there's a serious problem that goes beyond being late due to unforeseen circumstances.

Punctuality is a Lifestyle

We all have habits, some good and some bad. Lateness is a bad habit that a lot of people never really consider to be one, because they always have one explanation or the other for why they are late. They may apologize for being late this time, only to turn up late again another time in the not too distant future, armed with a brand-new excuse. A habitual late comer is like an alcoholic who believes he is in control of his liquor, but always ends up drunk. Being habitually late is not a lifestyle you should adopt and it needs to be curtailed, or it may lead to serious repercussions in both the short and long run. Being punctual in every single situation starts with a decision. It begins with your commitment to change from your bad habit and replacing it with a good one. Just like all bad habits, lateness can be tough to overcome and you will need to take deliberate steps in ensuring that you are always punctual and you never have to give any excuses for why you are late again.

It Starts with you

In reality, your ability to quit the habit of lateness, like all other habits, begins and ends with you. Only you can decide whether or not you want to be punctual. Like they say, you can lead a horse to water, but you can't make it drink. The decision is yours to make and if you decide to change your lateness habit, then this book will help you to fully understand why you are always late for every single occasion, even when you had planned on being there on time. It will let you in on proven practical steps you can take to develop the habit of being punctual, and also teach you how to maintain and perfect your new found lifestyle called punctuality!

CHAPTER 1

YOU ARE LATE!

Hi Honey, I'll be a Few Minutes Late

Have you ever been stood up by your significant other? You had planned a romantic evening a week before to celebrate your wedding anniversary, and it comprised of dinner at an exotic restaurant where you were meant to meet at a table reserved for two at precisely 8 PM. You got to the restaurant at about 7:15 PM and settled in, in anticipation of a wonderful meal and the pleasant company of your spouse. By 7:45 PM, you become agitated and you give your hubby a call. He tells you he's on his way and should be there soon. It's now 5 minutes after 8 PM and still your hubby is nowhere to be found. You endure and even order for a drink and fiddle with your mobile phone to kill time. Eventually, you begin to lose patience and you place another call at 8:30 PM. The call is unresponsive and now you get angry. By 9:10 PM, your hubby walks into the restaurant and tries frantically to pacify you, but you are not having it. You then ask the question, "Why are you late?" And his reply to your question is "I was stuck in traffic". Somehow, this explanation doesn't hold up and you respond with "That's been your excuse every year for the last five years' hon!" Ouch!!

This scenario may sound familiar to some couples and can really put a strain on any relationship. Being a habitual latecomer means that you are always late regardless of the event, occasion, situation or circumstance. There are differences between a punctual person, an occasional latecomer and a habitual latecomer. The striking difference between the three groups is in their ability or inability to keep to time. You should honestly know which group you belong to. That's the first step in knowing what you need to do to either keep up the lifestyle or change the bad habit.

1. Punctual as Always

A punctual person has embraced the nature of keeping to time, whether at work or at home. This individual will plan ahead of time in preparation for the scheduled appointment, and if the meeting is an impromptu one, punctual people will tell you when they can make it, and they will remain true to their word always. You can rely on punctual people, and if such a person doesn't show up for a scheduled appointment, then it could be a cause for worry as it is completely out of character. Such people increase their chances of success as they earn people's trust, confidence and goodwill. Being punctual also means completing tasks and obligations within a specific time frame. It means being on time for both important and not so important events and occasions. It is a lifestyle and a way of life that defines the way you handle issues, whether they are work related or personal in nature. It really doesn't matter to you, and you will be punctual in every situation as it is the life you have chosen to live.

2. The Occasionally Latecomer

An occasional latecomer is someone who may or may not deliberately decide to be late. Such a person is known for being relatively punctual, but at times, certain situations may cause the person to be late on occasion. Lateness of any form is not a good sign and it causes a dent in your character, but people that are occasionally late can get away with being late occasionally because people who know them are aware that there must be a reasonable excuse for why the person is running late. It helps your cause if you are able to communicate the fact that you will be a little late to the person or people you intend meeting with. However, if you are meeting this person or people for the first time, then your late coming will speak volumes about your character and could easily make them form a negative opinion about you before you meet with them. Occasional latecomers are lukewarm in their attitude and in their management of time. Sometimes they can be very good at using their time, then at other times, they are lousy. It is this inconsistency that can make them easily slide into becoming habitual latecomers.

3. The Habitual Latecomer

If you belong to this group, then you really need to take a critical look at yourself. For whatever reason, you always seem to be late for everything. Like the scenario painted earlier, you never seem to learn from your mistakes and you always have a ready excuse for why you are late, never once blaming yourself for your lateness. It has become a habit and the sad part is you don't even know it's a habit and you can't even comprehend how it is affecting your relationship with other people including your family, friends and colleagues. It is easy to get caught up in your own little world and forget that you are part of something much larger than you can imagine. Habitual latecomers would also never accept that they have a problem. They blame everything and everyone for their lateness. This makes them extremely difficult to convince and makes them difficult to convert into people that have embraced a punctual habit. They are easily get offended when you even mention the fact that they are responsible for their own lateness, and they have a stubbornness that quite frankly cannot be fully understood.

Punctuality vs. Lateness

By now you ought to know the difference between being punctual and being late, but just in case you are not yet convinced about the obvious difference, then a quick comparison of the two should help you tell the difference. I call this the **TIME** comparison. **TIME** is an acronym for;

T - Time

I - Issues

M - Me

E - Excuses

T - Time

You are always on time when you are the punctual type. You respect the time of others and you endeavor to meet up with appointments in accordance to the mutually agreed time. Latecomers unfortunately do not respect the time of others; it means nothing to them, and you really can't take their word for a fact. When it relates to scheduling a meeting or an appointment with them, they will be late or worse still, they may not even show up. Time to a person that has embraced a punctual lifestyle is sacrosanct. It is not something that should be toyed with or taken for granted. Every little thing is tied to time, like waking up from bed, taking a bath, brushing your teeth and so on. Every second matters and is used judiciously. Latecomers care less about when they wake up, when they have their bath and when they brush their teeth. Time is of no consequence to them and they could care less about it.

I - Issues

When you are punctual, you don't create issues for yourself or others. However, your late coming can create minor to severe problems for you and for other people including your family, friends and colleagues. When you are a perennial latecomer, you always seem to have the habit of eating into other people's time and that is because you don't regard your own time and that of others. This creates problems for other people because they could have used their valuable time in doing something more productive. Instead, they have to spend time dealing with the problems you might have created.

M - Me

People that keep to time care about others. They respect and appreciate the time and effort made by others and they do everything possible to maintain a good relationship with other people. Being punctual is one very good way of improving your relationship with others and building trust. Punctual people are selfless and would willingly sacrifice their time and comfort if it would help others. However, for latecomers, it's all about them. The "me" factor is high with them and that makes them insensitive to the time and effort of other people. They can be quite selfish and will always look out for their own interests, even if it means infringing on that of others.

E - Excuses

Latecomers always have one excuse or another for being late. Their excuses can be somewhat reasonable or out rightly ludicrous. For punctual people, excuses are just lame. They take responsibility for their action or inaction, and they don't go blaming anything or anyone for their shortcomings. For latecomers, it is never their fault for being late. "It's the weather", "its bad traffic", "it's a toothache", it's this and that... One excuse after another and the sad part is the excuses always seem to be prepared beforehand, almost as if they knew they would be late.

Now ask yourself, which side of the divide do you belong; the punctual or latecomers' side. If you are a punctual person, then good for you and you really should keep it up. However, if you are a latecomer, then I seriously advise that you finish reading this book and hopefully, you would move from your habitual lateness to being a punctual person.

CHAPTER 2

LATE YET AGAIN!

Why you're always Late

If you are reading this, then I assume you have done some self-assessment and realized that you need to change and drop your habit of being late. Now that you know the difference between being punctual and being late, you need to understand the reasons behind your habitual lateness before you can begin the process of readjusting to a more preferred lifestyle in which you are always punctual. There are five critical reasons why you are always late that will be examined in this chapter and they include the following;

1. Poor Time Management
2. Scheduling an Appointment, you can't Meet
3. Forgetfulness
4. Unnecessary Distraction
5. No Contingency Plan

1. Poor Time Management

Coming in at number one for the reasons why you are always late is poor time management. This reason is one that should be taken really seriously because it is actually the major reason why you are never punctual. First of all, it is important to know what time management is and the simplest explanation is your ability to prioritize the activities you perform in an hour, a day, a week or even a month. Time management requires that you use your time wisely and basically set out time for each activity.

So, What's the Problem?

The problem with most perennial latecomers is that they just don't know how to prioritize their activities and set out appropriate time for each of them. When you do not use your time properly, you are more than likely to spend more time than necessary on a particular task or activity. For example, you resume for work by 8 AM, but you need to be out of your home by 7 AM in order to meet up. However, you spent last night working and only slept in the early hours of the morning, which led to you waking up by

6:45 AM, leaving you with just 15 minutes to prepare for work. With proper time management, you will be able to get a grip of your tasks and activities and none would conflict with the other. Good time management will ensure that you are punctual to work and all other activities and tasks at all times.

Manage your Time Effectively

To be able to manage your time effectively, you will need to follow these ten (10) simple steps.

- Step 1 - Get yourself a personal diary.

- Step 2 - List out your daily tasks or activities in the order of their priority.

- Step 3 - Assign a time frame for each task or activity.

- Step 4 - Put the time frame to the test by applying it.

- Step 5 - Be consistent with the time frame for a week.

- Step 6 - Review your activities for the week and see if the time frame assigned to each task or activity was realistic or not.

- Step 7 - Adjust the time frame for each task or activity accordingly and apply it for the following week.

- Step 8 - Add new tasks and activities as they present themselves and assign time frames to each.

- Step 9 - Review and readjust the time frame once more and apply the modified time frame the following week.

- Step 10 - Practice, practice and more practice.

When you regularly try out these 10 simple steps, you will soon see improvements in your use of time which will be more efficient.

2. Scheduling an Appointment you can't Meet

For some reason, people have a habit of scheduling an appointment that they would not be able to honor. This habit can be traced to the same old issue of poor time management. If you had a clear understanding of your time, then you would know when to schedule an appointment. You will also know if you can make an event or not. The purpose of the time management diary is to serve as a guide or your very own personal assistant, to remind you of your daily tasks and obligations. It however doesn't mean that you cannot make adjustments to it if the need arises. Ultimately, its goal is to keep you on track as you make a conscious effort to use your time properly. To solve the problem of scheduling an appointment you will fail to meet, always refer to your diary to know if you can make out time for the appointment or not. It's all about prioritizing. If the meeting or event is very important, then it moves up the ladder of your list of priorities, while some other activity or task gets to move down the ladder to make room for the scheduled meeting or event. It's that simple, and you can't really go wrong when you try out this procedure as you will get to be punctual for the scheduled event or meeting you have prioritized.

3. Forgetfulness

We all forget to do stuff from time to time, that's quite normal, but when you forget a very important event or occasion, like your wedding anniversary or your kid's birthday, then you have serious forgetfulness issues. Now I'm not saying you have a serious medical condition like permanent amnesia or Alzheimer's disease. However, you need to seriously consider why you just can't seem to remember memorable events and occasions, let alone scheduled meetings and appointments. Whatever the reason for your forgetfulness, you can do yourself a whole lot of good by documenting every event or occasion in your diary according to their scheduled date. You could also do this on your smartphone as well. However, I prefer you write it down on paper. It may seem old fashioned, but it works like a charm if you want to remember stuff. Once you are able to remember important events and occasions, you improve your chances of honoring them when they are due.

4. Unnecessary Distraction

One way to forget to meet up with an appointment or be late for an event is when you are distracted. Distractions are everywhere, both at work or at home. They can cause you to lose track of your priorities and when you do, you become less time conscious and this can lead to lateness. Try to stay true with your priorities and do things in moderation; Watch less television, spend less time on your computer or on your mobile devices. Anything that will take your attention away from your priorities, you need to control them. When you do, you will see vast improvements in your ability to promptly meet your scheduled tasks and activities.

5. No Contingency Plan

The last but by no means the least of the reasons why you tend to be habitually late is because you have no contingency plan. Having a plan "B" will help you to be punctual and save you a lot of frustration. Imagine a scenario where you need to attend your son's baseball game at a park in 45 minutes. The game is scheduled to hold during rush hour and you know that if you drive, you will get stuck in traffic even though it will only take you about 35 minutes to reach the park. However, there is a second alternative which involves you taking the subway and spending just 15 minutes of your time on the train. It will take you another 15 minutes to walk to the park from the subway to watch the game, leaving you with 15 minutes of time to spare, as well as a very happy boy. By the way, your vehicle is safely parked in your office parking lot, so no worries. This is just one scenario that explains how you can manage your time well by having a contingency plan, thinking ahead, exploring all the options and possibilities, and looking for the best one that will optimize the use of your time and effort.

CHAPTER 3

YOU HAD IT COMING!

What Goes Around...?

If you believe in karma, then you will have to believe that if you are a habitual latecomer for important and not so important occasions and events, it will eventually catch up with you. You might be wondering what exactly would "catch up" with you. Well, for starters, your reputation. Most people prefer relating with others they consider as serious minded individuals. When you are habitually late for anything, you are not taken seriously. You would have gotten away with being a latecomer in your youth, but as an adult, your reputation precedes you. Even when you decide to make a positive change and you actually take the appropriate steps to improve your punctuality, a negative impression about you has already been formed in the minds of those people that know you, and you will have a lot of work to do convincing them otherwise, as well as letting them know that you are now a changed person. However, if you continue with the habit of lateness even as an adult, then you are exposed to far reaching consequences.

Drawbacks of Habitual Lateness

When you have perfected the unfortunate act of appearing late for virtually every event in your life, you will be left to rue your decision and you will have nothing and no one to blame but yourself. By being a habitual latecomer, you are exposed to quite a number of unpleasant situations that could have been avoided if you had taken your time to be more organized and time conscious. Four notable drawbacks of your habitual lateness are:

1. Credibility issues

2. Missed memories

3. Missed opportunities

4. Strained relationships

These four broad demerits of being a habitual latecomer should not be taken for granted. When you consider each drawback in more detail, you will fully understand how your lateness affects both you and other people, as well as how it can seriously sour your relationship with others and make you miss out on great opportunities.

1. Credibility Issues

If there is one thing that is more valuable than your life, it has to be your reputation. Most people spend a lifetime building and maintaining their reputation because they know that their legacy lives on even after they are dead and buried. Your reputation is what defines you. It is who you are in the heart and minds of other people, including your family, friends and colleagues. One way to enhance your reputation is by being punctual. People respect and admire this quality because it means that you are reliable and this builds trust. When people know that you can be trusted to be punctual, they can vouch for you even under completely unrelated circumstances, simply because they have a good impression of you. However, when you are a perpetual latecomer, it affects the way you are perceived by people. You are seen as untrustworthy and unreliable. No one would want to stick their neck out for you because it's just too risky doing so. They know you can be trusted to disappoint and so they are not surprised when you do. If you ever have a need for a guarantor, you could have trouble getting one because of your unsavory reputation for late coming, which in the mind of your would-be guarantor, translates to insincerity and unreliability. You lose credibility fast when you maintain the nasty habit of being late in everything you do.

2. Missed Memories

There is nothing more frustrating to your loved ones than you not showing up for an important occasion in their lives. Missing your daughter's high school graduation ceremony or missing your son's soccer game can have you missing out on memories that can never be replaced. When a photo album is flipped open and memories are being shared amongst family members, that is when it hits home hard, that you have missed out on events that should have cemented your relationship with your family members or the person or people concerned. By being punctual to events and occasions that are important to others, you are telling them without even uttering a word that you care about their happiness and you love them enough to sacrifice your time to be there for them. With being habitually late, you miss out on a number of events that you shouldn't have and this can create a wedge in your relationship with others.

3. Missed Opportunities

When you arrive late for virtually every event or occasion, you increase your chances of missing out on opportunities that may arise. The old saying of an early bird catching the fattest worm comes to mind. Whether it's a business opportunity or an opportunity to leave a lasting first impression in the heart and mind of your date, by being late for a scheduled meeting of any kind, you are likely to make it easy for the person or people you were meant to meet with to decide and form an opinion of you. If you show up pretty late for a first date, your date may be reluctant to go out on a second date with you, as you didn't make a good first impression. A lucrative business partnership could be called-off due to your inability to keep to time.

4. Strained Relationships

You will improve your relationship with family, friends and colleagues when you are punctual all the time. However, if you make it a habit to show up late for work, to a family occasion or a business meeting, you can cause a strain in your relationship with others. People tend to get irritated by someone who seemingly wastes their time, and if you are consistent at being late and people around you are aware of this fact, you are more likely to have less friends and more soured relationships with family members. Your kids for example could feel like you don't care about them and that is why you are always late to events that are very important in their lives. This could cause them to become rebellious and act out their anger and frustration in different negative ways.

Stop Being Late!

Habitual lateness has the potential to ruin reputations and relationships. It is surprising that a lot of people can't see this and make deliberate attempts to be punctual in all they do, when it's so obvious that they are losing credibility amongst their family, friends and colleagues. Make a conscious effort to be on time today and watch as your relationship with others dramatically improves.

CHAPTER 4

A QUICK INTROSPECTIVE LOOK

Everyone seems to have one reason or the other for why they are always late. Some explanations are more reasonable than others. However, in reality, all are just excuses. You need to take a step back and ask yourself the simple question of what keeps you from being punctual. This self-examination is your first step towards change. It is a sincere assessment of a flaw in your character that needs to be addressed. It starts with you examining situations and instances where you have been late and finding out why you were late. Most times, the reasons are quite simple and they can all be linked to your time management. However, you need to simplify these reasons and categorize them in accordance with the situation. For example, the reason why you are usually late for work could be due to poor time management occasioned by bad sleeping habits, such as sleeping late in the night or in the early hours of the morning, which causes you to wake up late in preparation for work. By specifying the actual cause of your lateness in the context of the overall reason which is ultimately poor time management, you are better able to deal with the problem.

It's the Small Stuff that Counts

When you address the small stuff, you eventually will solve the underlying problem. Like they say, the devil is in the detail. So, you have to be quite honest and critical about what you do or don't do. Dealing with the little issues is very important. If for example, you have the tendency to be late for work quite often because you don't sleep at the right time, but instead, you preoccupy yourself and your time with other distractions like watching a late-night TV show or working on your computer. If you want to wake up at a good time and adequately prepare for work, you would have to do without these distractions. By simply reducing the amount of time you spend watching TV or working on your computer late at night, you will be able to get more hours of quality sleep that would get you revitalized in the morning, and you would be able to consistently wake up early. By altering your lifestyle a bit, you can make definite strides in improving your punctuality.

Personal Reasons that Affect your Punctuality

If you have punctuality issues and you have taken an introspective look at what is personally responsible for your lateness, you will realize that it is due to some factors that we all take for granted. While ultimately poor time management is what leads to lateness, what causes you to badly manage your time is much more subtle. Here are five (5) reasons responsible for your poor time management.

1.   Bad habits

2.   Laziness

3.   Self-indulgence

4.   Procrastination

5.   Tiredness

1. Bad Habits Die Hard!

The problem most people face is that they don't view certain actions they take as bad habits. They are too caught up in the activity and cannot be reasoned with. One bad habit people have is not being time-conscious. You can wear a wristwatch or have an accurate wall clock available to you at all times, you could also set the alarm on your mobile phone, if it will get you to be aware of the time and be punctual. When you do this, there would be no more exclamations like "oh my, look at the time!"

2. Laziness to Lateness!

Some people are always late for the simple age old reason that they are lazy. Laziness can take many forms, for example, you could be lazy getting out of bed. You had set your alarm for 5 AM and it goes off, you want to be ready for work by 7 AM, so you decide to go back to bed as you believe you have at least an hour to spare, you then wake up by 7:15 AM. This is a common problem with most latecomers and it takes real commitment to be able to overcome. You can combat laziness by sleeping earlier than you might be used to, the night before. This way you will get more hours of quality sleep and wake up feeling refreshed and ready for the tasks ahead.

3. Self-indulgence for Me!

One other reason why you might be late most times is because you are a little selfish. It's all about you and your interests, your feelings, your this and your that! When you are too into yourself, you forget to do the little things that show that you care about others. You are too preoccupied with what you want and you are not willing to share your time with anyone except it will enhance your interests of course. You need to lose the ego and narcissism if you want to build relationships, especially with your loved ones. You can attend to the needs of others without it infringing on yours, if you plan your time well.

4. Procrastination Means No Action!

When you put things off till a later time, you could over burden yourself with too much work than you can handle, and as a result, you forget about every other thing. You could also form a nasty habit of mixing self-indulgence and procrastination, a very toxic mix that would only result in you prioritizing your activities and appointments based strictly on how it will be of benefit to you. So for example, if you are meant to show up for a PTA meeting, you would rather go and watch a football game and decide to attend the subsequent meeting. The only problem with this is you will always have something to preoccupy your time when the subsequent meeting is due. Your time will be strictly hinged on activities that will be personally beneficial to you and nothing else matters. You need to show more maturity and be less self-indulgent. Also, try to do things at the right time in order to avoid piling up tasks and commitments that cannot all be handled at the same time.

5. Tiredness Leads to Lateness!

You could be genuinely exhausted both physically and mentally. This can make you late for scheduled appointments and other commitments. To avoid being tired all the time, you can try to pace yourself at work and take a well-deserved vacation. You should also eat a balanced diet always and never miss breakfast as it is the most important meal of the day and it gets your energy levels up. Make sure to take breaks when you are tired; do not over exert yourself. Tiredness can make you less productive at work and you will actually be doing yourself more harm than good if you push yourself too hard. It will also lead to punctuality issues as well, so rest and eat well to keep tiredness at bay.

CHAPTER 5

A CALL TO ACTION

Less Talk, More Action!

It's time to talk less and spend more time and effort being punctual. Punctuality is a good habit you need to adopt today and like all good habits, you get better at it with practice, and in due time, it becomes a lifestyle. However, to be able to make punctuality a part and parcel of your everyday life, you will need to do certain things on a consistent basis. Here's a list of ten (10) things you should regularly do if you want to be consistently punctual.

1. Sleep early
2. Don't eat late
3. Set your alarm
4. Keep a diary
5. Do things while they are fresh in your memory
6. Don't spend too much time on irrelevant activities
7. Delegate responsibilities more
8. Take breaks when tired
9. Mentally plan out your day
10. Allot a specific time frame to each task

1. Sleep Early

Sleep is great for rejuvenating your body and when you get quality sleep by sleeping for a minimum of eight (8) hours daily, you will be physically strong and mentally alert all through the day. However, for you to get quality sleep, you will need to sleep early the night before. You can sleep by 9 PM but not later than 10 PM daily. This way, you will wake up feeling refreshed and ready for the tasks ahead of you, and your renewed energy and mental focus will ensure that you are punctual more often than usual.

2. Don't Eat Late

Eating dinner is good, but you should try and have your dinner on or before 8 PM. Try not to eat heavy meals late at night, as it will cause you to be restless during the night, and this will adversely affect your quality of sleep. It can also lead to digestive issues like indigestion and constipation, which further makes you uncomfortable and grumpy during the day. When you don't get sufficient sleep, you are less physically prepared and mentally focused for your daily tasks, and you become more prone to procrastination and lateness.

3. Set your Alarm

If you want to be punctual for work, you can set your alarm clock for the time you would want to wake up. You can also set your alarm to remind you of the times when you have important appointments to meet. An alarm clock in your bedroom and on your bedside table is a useful accessory. Also, using the alarm of your mobile phone can help remind you of scheduled tasks and commitments, so that you are always on time in meeting them.

4. Keep a Diary

This might be a bit old school in these days of digital schedulers on your mobile devices, but whether you use a diary and pen or your digital scheduler, the bottom line is, make sure you have a way of noting important events and planning towards them. Once these events are written down or typed in, they register in your mind as very important. You would have prioritized them and you will be reluctant to miss out on such occasions and events. Having a diary will help you to be punctual.

5. Do Things While they are Fresh in your Memory

When you perform tasks immediately rather than put them off for a later date, you improve your control of your time. When tasks are piled up, it becomes difficult for you to manage your time and you will be more susceptible to being overworked, tired and less likely to be punctual at other important activities.

6. Don't Spend too much Time on Irrelevant Activities

You should spend less time on activities that can be set aside for a later date. If you prioritize irrelevant activities, you only make the relevant ones less important. When you spend too much time watching TV or playing video games, you are bound to lose track of time and be late for that important event, task or activity. Always do things in moderation; never spend too much time doing activities that have no direct positive bearing on your life.

7. Delegate Responsibilities More

Do not try to do everything yourself, you will only wear yourself out. Delegate more responsibility to others and take the load off your chest. When you delegate responsibilities, you increase the time available to you, reduce stress and improve your punctuality in the process.

8. Take Breaks when Tired

Whenever you are physically and mentally exhausted, take a short break. When you do this, you will rejuvenate yourself and get your energy levels up. Your concentration will equally improve and you will be sharper in thought and action. If you need an extended break from your work activities, you can go on a holiday. Never overwork yourself as this is a recipe for both physical and mental breakdown.

9. Mentally Plan out your Day

Before the start of each day, you need to make a mental note of all the tasks you have planned out ahead of you. Think about how you intend executing the tasks and just plan out your entire day in your mind by painting a mental picture of how you are going to carry them out. This will prepare you mentally for the tasks ahead and you will also be able to know if you are ready to execute them or not. You will be able to motivate yourself this way, and it will make you more conscious of the time available to you and how you should go about utilizing it.

10. Allot a Specific Time Frame to Each Task

You should make sure to allot a specific time frame to each task you perform. When you do this, you are likely to avoid spending an excessive amount of time on each task. You become more organized and that means your punctuality will also improve. Make sure you keep to the time frame you have created and don't renege on it. It will ensure that you manage your time better and your punctuality will generally be better.

Take Action!

Action speaks louder than words, so try out these ten (10) tips to ensure that you are always punctual in all that you do. Start executing them today and the more you do, the better your punctuality will become. Practice makes perfect, so keep practicing and you will be glad you did.

CHAPTER 6

EUREKA!

Success, Success...

You have been able to tick all the boxes in your daily tasks and commitments for a whole week. A visit to the dentist by 4 PM on Tuesday - check! A romantic dinner with your partner by 7 PM on Wednesday to celebrate a promotion - check! A meeting with a potential business partner by 2 PM on Friday - check!!! Every possible commitment and obligation has been met because you took time out to be organized and to manage your time better. With each box you tick, there is an immediate feeling of accomplishment that comes with it, no matter how insignificant the task or activity may be. The moment it is done and in accordance with your plan and within your set time frame, you are elated and your desire to fulfill more tasks and obligations only heightens. It is the unmistakable feeling that success brings, where you just want to stand out in an open field and yell out eureka! Eureka!!

The Road to Success

The road to your time management and punctuality success is never easy, as old habits always seem too rear their ugly head to stall your plans. However, it is all about perseverance and perfecting the art of being punctual. You start with the little stuff, those commitments that may not seem very important, but they actually are if you want to have and maintain a viable lifestyle of being on time every time. Picking your kids from school at an exact time or helping out with the groceries on certain days may seem harmless enough, but if you can get these little seemingly simple tasks done within your proposed time frame, then you will improve your chances of achieving more difficult obligations on time when they arise. You need to keep at being punctual and don't relent. Once you make it a habit, you will be on time for every single activity regardless of its importance.

Benefits of Being Punctual

Now that you know why you are always late and how you can become more punctual in all that you do, you should also know the benefits of being on time as this should spur you on to improve on your punctuality. The merits of punctuality far outweigh the drawbacks of being late, and they have a positive effect on you as well as those around you. You can benefit from being punctual in these five (5) ways;

- Better relationships
- Increased goodwill
- Self-satisfaction
- More opportunities
- Better time management

1. Better Relationships

As you improve on your punctuality, your relationship with other people equally improves. Your family, friends and colleagues will welcome your new found change and their perception of you will start to change gradually. The onus is on you to be consistent with being punctual. At first, people may be surprised by the change and a little skeptical of the fact that it is a permanent change in your lifestyle. They would want to watch you for some time before finally accepting the fact that you have changed for real. Some may be waiting for you to live up to your earlier reputation of being a latecomer, while some would be cautiously optimistic about your change, and yet others would be happy and hope that it continues.

2. Increased Goodwill

When you embrace punctuality, you leave yourself open to a lot of goodwill from family, friends and colleagues. People naturally gravitate towards those that are dependable and trustworthy. By improving on your punctuality, people will begin to trust you and open up to you on a number of issues that would be of tremendous benefit to you. Trust brings about openness, so learn to be punctual in order to earn the trust of family and friends. This way, you will receive more goodwill from them.

3. Self-satisfaction

Punctuality is like a tonic for your ego; nothing can be more satisfying than knowing that you were on time for an important occasion in the lives of family and friends. The feeling you get from being on time also lifts your spirits and your self-confidence will increase. This is especially good and necessary if you are meeting for a job interview. Your self-esteem will go through the roof when you are punctual and you will be able to scale through the job interview successfully.

4. More Opportunities

You can't go wrong when you are on time for something. Your punctuality can open up doors of opportunities for you. In your career, business and even love life, by being on time for something, you actually boost your chances of being successful at it. A classic case of the early bird catching the fattest worm if you like, but when it comes to punctuality, this old saying has some genuine truth to it.

5. Better Time Management

With your punctuality improving, it only means that your time management skills are better. You are better able to prioritize your tasks and commitments in a way that you can optimize the limited time available to you to fulfill all your required activities. This should be your punctuality goal and it is also a major benefit. Time waits for no one, but you can effectively manage it and get the best out of it.

Be in Control

Don't allow both external and internal factors like bad weather, poor traffic, car trouble or even sickness get in your way of being punctual all the time. You should be the master of your time and be in full control of it. While there are genuine circumstances that would hamper your ability to effectively manage your time and be punctual in all you do, it should not stop you from having a contingency plan for dealing with such situations if and when they arise. Give a thought to almost every scenario that could stop you from fulfilling your obligations and find solutions to each. By doing this, you are reducing your tendency to be late at something and at the end of the day, you are better off for it.

CHAPTER 7

STAYING ON TRACK

Stay Punctual

Punctuality, as you know by now, is far better than being late. However, you should also know that staying punctual has always been much more difficult once you have adopted it as your new way of life. This is when the hard work begins. This is when you need to be on your guard to ensure that your punctuality is maintained and not a one-off occurrence. Once you have embraced this lifestyle and you are committed to maintaining it, you will need to do certain things and take certain steps that will help you stay punctual and keep you from sliding back into your previous habit of being late in virtually everything you do.

How to Maintain Punctuality

Maintaining a punctual lifestyle requires that you show certain behavioral traits that will keep you completely focused on showing up on time in all that you do. Here are ten (10) characteristics that are expected from you if you want to sustain your punctuality lifestyle.

1.	Hard work	6.	Maturity
2.	Focus	7.	Consistency
3.	Determination	8.	Self-discipline
4.	Commitment	9.	Self confidence
5.	Composure	10.	Self-improvement

1. Hard work

Once you have adapted to being punctual in all you do, you need to put in a lot of hard work in ensuring that you remain punctual and you do not regress. Hard work means continuous practice. Being punctual should be part and parcel of what you do and who you are. It should be part of your DNA and you should apply it in everything; you should be punctual for a meal, for work, for an engagement and so on. When you make being punctual for all your activities a must, it will come naturally to you, but you need to put in the work in order to perfect it.

2. Focus

Punctuality requires you to be 100% focused on the tasks in hand. You need to understand what you need to do to meet up with the activity and the time it would take you to achieve it. When you are focused on all your tasks in the order of their priority, you will be willing and ready to sacrifice little comforts to ensure that you are on time in order to accomplish the tasks and see them through to their logical conclusion.

3. Determination

One trait that is absolutely crucial to you being punctual always is determination. Without determination, you cannot maintain your punctual lifestyle. It is determination that keeps you going despite the situation you find yourself in. Even when you are exposed to a tremendous amount of stress, with determination, you will be able to overcome the situation and maintain your punctuality no matter what. It is determination that stops you from giving excuses when you are late. No matter your personal problems, you will be on time every time and see the task or obligation through.

4. Commitment

You have started something good, now you need to stay committed to it. It's the only way that you can maintain your punctuality. Just like determination, commitment will keep you from falling back into old habits. You don't want to be punctual this week then revert to your old habit of being late next week. You need to stay true to the new path you are on and steady the course through good times and bad.

5. Composure

This is a very important personal trait to have. When you are calm under pressure, you react to situations better and act accordingly based on wise thought and better judgment. When you do not panic when things are not going your way, you will always find a solution. If for example you are running late for a wedding because your car won't start, getting unnecessarily worried and panicking will only make you take rash and irrational decisions. However, remaining calm and composed will help you to make a well thought of and informed decision that will help you show up for the wedding on time despite the fact that your car won't start.

6. Maturity

You have to exhibit a level of maturity when you are trying to be consistently punctual. Maturity entails that you are always planning on how you can improve your level of time management and be better at using the time available to you. It encompasses several other traits such as composure, self-discipline, personal improvement and focus. It is maturity that ensures that you are not overwhelmed with obligations that wear you out mentally and physically, but rather, you are able to allot sufficient time to each task and obligation in order to see them accomplished.

7. Consistency

This is a key behavioral trait that is needed if you are to maintain your punctuality. You cannot be on a roller coaster ride when it comes to punctuality. You cannot be punctual one minute and then late the next. Your consistency is what builds trust with other people because they know what to expect from you. You are not topsy-turvy, but steady and seemingly predictable. This increases your reliability and people are happier dealing with someone that is dependable and not erratic.

8. Self-discipline

Just like maturity, you also need lots of self-discipline. You cannot over indulge yourself in irrelevant activities at the expense of more serious ones. Your list of priorities and their respective time frames should be your number one concern; every other thing should take the back seat. There is no point in you spending so much time watching TV for example, when you had tasks you could have accomplished in the same time period. By not showing enough self-discipline, it can cause you to procrastinate quite a lot, leading to your work load piling up and increasing your risk of being late in fulfilling your assignments.

9. Self Confidence

Maintaining your punctuality requires that you are sure of yourself and you have confidence in your time management plan and decision. Self-confidence is important if you want to always be punctual, but this should not be mistaken for arrogance. Self-confidence is just the self-assurance in your ability to be organized and keep at being punctual. It also means that you are open to change and flexible enough to make the necessary adjustments in order to maintain your punctuality. Arrogance on the other hand is a blind pride in which you are not open to change and valuable suggestions on how you can improve yourself in order to maintain your punctuality. Instead, you are full of yourself and you think you have mastered the control of your time and punctuality when in fact you are yet to. Try to be flexible to change and improvement, always look for better solutions to ensuring that your punctuality is maintained and does not drop in consistency, and avoid complacency brought about by arrogance.

10. Self-Improvement

When you are open to positive change through self-improvement, you will get better at maintaining your punctuality. It means you are working hard at being punctual and you are not satisfied with your present punctuality, as you recognize that it can only get better. Self-improvement is holistic and involves you working on every characteristic mentioned earlier and improving on each of them in order for you to be the best person possible because you know that if you work hard, you are composed, determined and committed. You have self-discipline as well as focus and maturity, then, you will be able to manage your time even better and stay punctual always.

Keep at it

Try as hard as you can develop the ten (10) characteristics mentioned in this chapter. When you work on them, your time management skills will surely improve and you will be punctual more often than not. These personal traits need to be constantly developed, so don't get complacent even when your punctuality has improved. Keep working at it and you will be better off for it.

CHAPTER 8

THE NEW YOU

Perfecting the Lifestyle Called Punctuality

Your new found lifestyle is bound to set you apart from the rest of the crowd as a reliable, dependable and responsible person. Your relationship with your family, friends and colleagues will improve because of the trust you have earned just by being punctual in your relationship with them. Punctuality is not just appearing for a scheduled meeting or appointment on time. It also involves meeting deadlines, like in the submission of a thesis or assignment. It must be reflected in everything you do, that is why it is a lifestyle. Your punctuality is a reflection of who you are and how you want to live your life. It defines you and guides you at the same time. Maintaining this lifestyle is no easy task and requires a continuous assessment of where, what and who you are. It is a daily commitment to excellence, a focus and determination that is unrivaled and a maturity beyond your years. Once you make punctuality an everyday routine, you will reap its benefits and you will never want to go back to your previous unenviable habit of lateness. You will continue to push towards perfection and self-improvement while ensuring consistency and continuity in your new found punctuality lifestyle.

No One does it Better

The number one rule in punctuality is your time management. It is your time and no one can spend it for you; you get to decide how you want to use it. No matter what advice you get from family, friends and colleagues on how you should use your time, ultimately the burden rests with you and only you can decide what, when and how to use your time. You are the master of your destiny and that destiny is intertwined with your time. Therefore, you have to use it wisely and when you do, you will realize that punctuality will form the basis of your time management, as that essentially is what time management is all about. It's all about you using the time available to you in the most efficient way possible, which would mean you will waste less time in achieving your tasks and doing so within the time frame you have allotted for each of the tasks and obligations available to you. No one can manage your time better than you. So with constant practice and the execution of your time management plan, you will maintain a level of punctuality that is worthy of emulation.

Get Better at Doing the Little Things

When you are extremely good at achieving the little things, like waking up from bed at a particular time or eating your meals at a set time, then you will transmit this trait to being punctual in achieving bigger things. It becomes a part of you and though it may seem regimented, it is a self-discipline that you need to have in order to be punctual. Without self-control, you will never be consistent at being punctual. You will always have a cat and mouse relationship with punctuality. By mastering the art of being punctual in the little things, you will build the confidence to be punctual in more complicated tasks and obligations. You take small steps towards bigger goals and at the end of the day, you will be better off for it.

Personal Improvement

As you become more and more in tune with your new lifestyle, you will notice great improvements in your personality. You will not be the same person you were in the past. Those habits that adversely affected your punctuality are now a thing of the past and you are a more mature and accomplished person at managing your time and being punctual in all that you do. You have more self-confidence and self-belief in your time management skills, and you have backed this confidence with focus and determination in ensuring its consistency. Personal improvement is key for you to keep up your punctuality lifestyle. It is the difference between a one-off and a consistent level of punctuality. As you work hard at developing yourself, you will set the bar high and this will ensure that you achieve a consistent level of punctuality in all that you do.

Have a Plan "B"

If your first plan at being punctual at something doesn't work out as planned, switch to your plan "B". It is important as you mature in managing your time and being consistently punctual that you develop alternate plans to execute each task or obligation. This is important just in case your original plan does not materialize. Having a contingency plan helps to keep you calm under pressure, especially when you know you have an option if all things fail. However, for you to develop a plan "B", you will need to give the entire assignment some serious thought. It is only then that you will be able to come up with viable solutions that could be implemented if your preferred option doesn't work out. This comes with a level of consistency garnered over time.

Live your Life

Most importantly, you need to live your life at the end of the day and in doing so, make sure that you have time for less serious engagements provided they don't interfere with the time you have allotted in achieving your priorities. Have fun when you have to and be less strict with your time spent on having fun. This will help to get you relaxed and you will be less on edge. You can take a day out of the seven days in a week as your day to unwind and have fun. On this day, you do not have to worry too much about being punctual in meeting obligations as the only obligation you have is to yourself and family. Go out with family and friends and live your life on this day. It will give a balance to your life and get you refreshed to tackle the tasks ahead of you. Nothing helps you perform better than when you are rejuvenated and well rested. So sleep well, eat well and play well on this off day from your regular strict regimen.

CONCLUSION

The Ball is in your Court

After all is said and done, the onus rests with you to be punctual in all that you do. It is a decision you have to take and one that will affect the rest of your life. Punctuality starts with your attitude. If you are not willing to put in the required level of hard work, commitment, determination, focus, self-discipline and maturity needed to churn out a consistent level of punctuality week in, week out then you cannot sustain this lifestyle, no matter what anyone tells you. You have the power to either improve on your time management skills or to maintain your lifestyle of being late at most things you do. Whatever choice you make, you can be sure that your decision will have a lasting effect on your life whether for good or for bad. You hold all the aces and you should use them wisely.

Dependable and Reliable

By choosing a punctual lifestyle, you will be viewed in a different light by those that know you. Though you were previously thought of as an unreliable and untrustworthy person, that is all in the past as you have now taken the right decision to make amends and be on the right path. When you meet new acquaintances, you will leave a lasting impression, and when you are with old friends and family, your new character will leave them amazed and gradually their opinion would start to change. The usual comments of "Oh, he's always late" or "He can't be trusted" will change to "He has changed" or "He's not the same person I used to know". Your new improved character will open up a lot of opportunities for you and all it took was for you to stop being a latecomer.

No More Lateness

It rests on you to maintain the same level of commitment in being punctual all through your lifetime. It is hard work, but when you apply it on a day to day basis, punctuality soon becomes a normal behavior for you. You will no longer have to worry about being late for anything because you will instinctively want to be punctual regardless of the circumstance. Consequently, whether you are meant to attend an important business meeting or you are supposed to be present at your child's baseball game, it's all the same to you. You will take each task as seriously as the next and endeavor to accomplish them on time. You have to make a promise to yourself that you would no longer be late for anything again, that you would strive to be punctual and give a 100% always in ensuring that you keep to a definite time frame in meeting all your tasks and obligations.

A Step to Greatness

With each obligation and task you achieve within the allotted time frame you have set out, you are moving a step closer to attaining your life objectives. Time waits for no man and it is short indeed. Subsequently, achieving your goals in life is actually the end result of your good time management and ability to fulfill every priority within their respective time frame. The better you are at ticking the boxes for each obligation and task achieved, the easier it would be for you to achieve your ambitions in life. Punctuality and attaining your life goals work hand-in-hand and are partners in progress. Most successful people have excellent time management skills and are punctual in all that they do. It is a lifestyle that they have adopted on their road to success and it has never failed them. If you also take this lifestyle on board, you are more than likely to be successful in whatever business or career path you choose.

Remember to Stay Grounded

There is always the tendency to be irritated and easily agitated by other people around you that may not necessarily share your convictions on punctuality. You are not living on a deserted Island, so you are bound to stumble upon people that are yet to embrace punctuality as a lifestyle. Do not act out on them and be cruel. Try to be understanding while still letting them know that their actions may affect others, yourself included.

Keep a level head and find other ways to meet up with your commitments without being overbearing and offensive. You have to show some maturity in the way you relate with other people and also show some respect, otherwise, people will see you as a pompous, self-serving and rude person. Even though this is not who you really are in reality, and you are just trying to make sure that your time is not wasted or taken for granted, other people won't see it this way. So, try to be accommodating and flexible with your time. Successful people have not only been able to manage their time, but they have also been able to manage people successfully as well.

Never Give Up

Just as life is a learning process and we all get to learn something new every day, so also is your punctuality lifestyle. You need to be patient with yourself while you take genuine strides towards achieving the consistency of your dreams. Rome wasn't built in a day and so also it is with this lifestyle. From the first day, you decide to be punctual, you have made a pact with yourself to endure and persevere in order to achieve your goals.

Mastering the art of punctuality takes time, so be prepared to work at it and don't get frustrated with yourself. With each improvement in your punctuality, you have taken a positive step in the right direction. Keep at it no matter what and you will eventually be rewarded for your hard work and commitment, but whatever you do - never give up!

Life is Good!

Life is so much better when you decide today to drop your lateness habit and switch to a punctual lifestyle. Apart from improved relationships, you also improve your physical and mental health. You become more active and less of a couch potato and your mind is always active as you think a lot on how to improve the use of your time. Psychologically, you have greater self-esteem as you are in better control of your time, and you use it in achieving your set priorities. Keep in mind that time is one thing that no one can control nor buy, so make sure that you spend your time wisely. Life has never been better than when you adopt a punctual lifestyle.

You Decide

Now that you know the importance of punctuality, I believe that if you have read this book to this point, you will take positive steps towards improving your lifestyle for the better. As long as you keep working on your punctuality, no matter how small of a change in your habit it may be, you will become a better version of yourself. However, if you choose to maintain your current lateness lifestyle over punctuality today, then I wish you all the best in perfecting the lifestyle called punctuality.

Kind regards,

Jeremy Bolton